Animal Antics

Debjani Chatterjee

Pennine Pens

Published 2000
Pennine Pens
32, Windsor Road, Hebden Bridge
West Yorkshire HX7 8LF
Tel 01422-843724
Fax 01422-847369
books@penninepens.co.uk
http://www.penninepens.co.uk
http://www.hebdenbridge.co.uk
in association with The Poetry Society

Copyright © Poems and illustrations Debjani Chatterjee 2000

All rights reserved

ISBN 1 873378 03 3

Classification: Poetry for children / Animals / English

Many of these poems were written while I was Poet-in-Residence at Sheffield Children's Hospital between January and July 2000. The residency was part of the Poetry Society's Poetry Places scheme, funded by the Arts Council of England's 'Arts for Everyone' budget. Most of these poems were also performed at the hospital. Some have been previously published in: *Big World, Little World* (Nelson), *Through A Window* (Longman), *The Word Party: A World Book Day Poetry Book* (Macmillan), *Unzip Your Lips Again: 100 More Poems To Read Aloud* (Macmillan), *Poems About School* (Wayland), *Albino Gecko* (University of Salzburg), *I Was That Woman* (Hippopotamus Press), *Smoke* and *Femina*. Some poems have been broadcast on the BBC. "The Elephant" won a Lancaster LitFest National Poetry Competition Prize. I am very grateful for the support and encouragement I have received from my husband, Brian D'Arcy, Christina Patterson at the Poetry Society, colleagues at Sheffield Children's Hospital Appeals Office and the Poet Laureate, Andrew Motion.

For my grandchildren:

*Jonathon, Sarah, Stephanie,
Matthew, Michael, Andrew,*

and

all the children at Sheffield Children's Hospital

Introduction to *Animal Antics*

Many of the poems in this energetic and beguiling book were written when Debjani Chatterjee was the Poet in residence attached to Sheffield Children's Hospital. Several of them confront the experience of fear and pain; several others celebrate healing and recovery. But whatever their subject, they confirm the salubrious power of poetry itself: its life-affirming rhythms, colours, movements and special ways of equipping us to deal with life in all its forms.

This is a heartening book, written by a poet full of wit and charm.

Andrew Motion
Poet Laureate

6th April 2000
London

CONTENTS

Introduction by Andrew Motion	4	Tomcat Jerry (a parody of 'Mrs Jaypher' by Edward Lear)	26
The Charming Wolf	6		
Please Save the Porcupine	6	The Monkey (a parody of 'The Tiger' by William Blake)	27
Rats in Hamlyn	7		
When the Beast Cried	7	Pride Shot	28
The Unicorn	8	Paper Tigers	29
Mermaid Masquerade	9	Mother and Child	30
Diwali	10	Proverbial Logic	30
An Epic Abridged	11	Cowboy Billy Joe	31
Dancing Ganapati	12	Riding High	32
Aching Bones	13	Squirreling	32
Jumbo Haiku Proverbs	14	My Rabbit is Magic	33
Elephant	14	Insects Rule	34
The Talking Parrot of Timbuktoo	15	Flat Share	35
		No Chrysalis	36
The Elephant	16	Study Subject	36
Jungle Truth	17	The Hippo	37
Snake in School	17	Astro-Turtle	39
What's for Dinner?	18	Wisdom Tooth	40
Comparing Pets	19	The Yeti	41
Boa Hugs	20	Anton, the Ant-eater	42
Like an Arm	20	Hanging Around	42
Vishnu's Eagle	21	Mela Menagerie	43
Hello, Mrs Magpie	22		
Feline Wiles	23		
The Cat Did It!	23	Helpful Hints	44
mouse	24	About the Poet	46
Mighty Mouse	25	Index of First Lines	47

The Charming Wolf

The wolf could talk
and it could sing:
it hypnotised Red Riding Hood.
The wolf could talk
and it could sing.
It chatted with her on her walk,
knew well how to pull her heart string -
she thought it much misunderstood.
They skipped and danced all through the wood.
The wolf could talk
and it could sing.

Please Save the Porcupine

In our school, Miss Meacher
is Cookery Teacher.
    She says that to dine
    upon porcupine
must quill the poor creature.

RATS IN HAMLYN

The Piper played
and charmed the rats who showed good taste.
The Piper played,
but human rats in Hamlyn stayed
to cheat him. In their greedy haste
they lost their children. Oh such waste!
The Piper played ...

WHEN THE BEAST CRIED

When the Beast cried
The Beauty's last defence was gone.
When the Beast cried
Innocence and Revulsion died.
With new insight she looked upon
His rough features. Her love was won
When the Beast cried.

THE UNICORN

Out of thunder
Earth asunder
Creature of fire
Born to inspire
A king of dreams
He rides moonbeams
Seeks to capture
All that's rapture
Tossing a horn
The unicorn
Wreaks his magic
Fabulogic

MERMAID MASQUERADE

Every ocean mermaid had come to masquerade:
The crazy and frantic ones from the Atlantic,
The frilly fantastic fish-girls of the Arctic,
The pretty terrific ones from the Pacific,
Dancers in slow motion from the Indian Ocean.
Every ocean was swum, every mermaid had come.
They were hale and hearty at fancy dress party.
Crawling sea slugs and prawns excited only yawns,
Baby dogfish would bark at the menacing shark,
And white horses galloped where seaweed was scalloped.
Neptune's fancy dress prize was for human disguise.

Diwali

Diwali lamps are twinkling, twinkling
In the sky and in our homes and hearts.
We welcome all with cheery greeting
And sweets and patterned *rangoli* art.
Lakshmi flies upon her owl tonight;
Incense curls, our future's sparkling bright.

An Epic Abridged

In *Ramayana*
    brave Rama Chandra,
        Prince of Ayodhya,
            was wed to Sita.
        Sita loved Rama,
    Rama loved Sita.
Demon Ravana,
    tyrant of Lanka,
        kidnapped sweet Sita.
            Monkeys helped Rama
        build from India
a bridge to Lanka,
They caused much brouha,
    beseiging Lanka,
        killing Ravana.
            Rama and Sita
        flew to Ayodhya
to shouts of "Hurrah!

Light every *diya*
    for Rama Chandra
        will be our Raja.
            Diwali hurrah!
    Rama and Sita,
back in Ayodhya!
Light every *diya*,
    throughout Ayodhya!
        Shout Hurrah! Hurrah!
            Jai Sita Rama!
        Hail Rama Sita!
    Jai Rama Sita!
Hail Sita Rama!"

Dancing Ganapati

Dancing Ganapati, trunk in the air,
we loved you and fed you on milk and sweets,
smeared sandal paste on your marble brow,
decked your pachyderm neck with fresh marigold,
beat on our drums and danced while you stared
with ears fanned out, for we hailed you in joy.
We waved oil lamps and swayed as we sang:
"Dancing Ganapati, trunk in the air,
bless us who worship with milk and sweets."

We slipped away, ate and drank in your name.
Life was as always: flesh-stoned together,
you were our friend, we knew where you stood.
Dancing Ganapati, trunk in the air,
we drank your milk and savoured your sweets
till the day you chose to take our treats -
we wondered where all the milk had gone,
and stared in disbelief at our old playmate:
dancing Ganapati, trunk in the milk!

ACHING BONES

There's nothing badder
    than an adder
        with aching bones.
            He moans and groans,
        and hisses and bites
    and gets into fights,
over nothing.
    So something
        has to be done for the adder
            or he gets badder and madder.
        But teach him some yoga,
    he'll sway like a cobra;
tying himself in knots,
    he'll think sweet thoughts.
        There's nothing gladder
            than an adder
        who owns
    flexible bones.

Jumbo Haiku Proverbs

In the elephant
orchestra, don't expect to
blow your own trumpet.

If you belittle
the elephant, prepare for
jumbo to squash you.

Elephant

All trunk, ears and legs,
its solid body confronts:
tusks at the ready.

THE TALKING PARROT OF TIMBUKTOO

I am the talking parrot of Timbuktoo;
I holler, I swear and I hullaballoo.
    The judge tried to fine me.
    I cursed him divinely,
So they shut me up behind bars in a zoo.

THE ELEPHANT

Elephants were not her cup of tea -
they were mammoth and boring,
immobile, they turned no somersaults.
Gaiety and the antics of monkeys
and insulting parakeets,
blinking and chattering,
offered her the warmth of fur and vivid feathers.
Elephants were distant, tusked and ominous.
Powerful and towering over children,
their long memories and wisdom
placed them in a different zoo for adults.
"But this is an Indian elephant,"
her father said. "It is homesick
and will cheer up to see an Indian girl
in this wet, cold, foreign land."
So she tore away from the noisy cages
and allowed herself to be slowly led
to greet her majestic compatriot.
She avoided those massive tree-trunk legs
and looked straight up at the eyes.
A storehouse of sorrow was locked in its brain.
Tentative, she reached out a hand and patted
the incredible trunk stretched out to her.

JUNGLE TRUTH

Mowgli grew up in the jungle,
A man among wolves was Mowgli.
When he went to find his own kind,
Wolves and jungle *were* the city.

SNAKE IN SCHOOL

One year in the Monsoon season
We all screamed and with good reason:
A water snake had come to school!
But Mister Singh just kept his cool.
He chased him out of our school gate
And told him off for being late!

Animal Antics

WHAT'S FOR DINNER?

Once a parrot and a goldfish
eyeballed each other in contest.
Polly said:" I spy a snack dish."
Goldie said:" You're a pesky pest."
A dog and cat were passing by
and baked them both into a pie.

COMPARING PETS

When mates boast about their hamsters,
gerbils and budgerigars, I smile.
When they harp on about their cats
and dogs, I find them juvenile.

Some take goats and chickens for walks,
others love goggle-eyed goldfish.
Some show off their spiders and frogs:
they're desperate to astonish.

My parents said no to monkeys,
hippos, crocodiles, wildebeeste.
"There's nowhere to keep them," they said.
But I'm not bothered in the least.

I take immense satisfaction,
knowing I have an elephant -
not quite a pet, more a tenant,
invisible under my bed!

Animal Antics

BOA HUGS

Noah is a boa constrictor,
A throttling, chortling, sumo wrestler.
His fangs are wicked, his grip awesome;
His belly ripples, dimples on bum,
Steely muscles down his scaly length,
All confirm his super champion's strength.
Coiled around, he will playfully squeeze;
Boa hugs make Noah the boas' knees!

LIKE AN ARM

It's like an arm:
Jumbo swats flies and shakes your hand.
It's like an arm,
that is the root of half its charm:
it's abracadabra and grand.
Jumbo's long trunk, you understand,
is like an arm.

Vishnu's Eagle

A sharp-beaked hunter of the chase,
Nemesis of the serpent race,
He scours the Earth, he straddles Space,

Spans the heavens with sturdy wings;
From worlds unseen, in glory brings
On his broad back the King of kings.

Hello, Mrs Magpie

Hello, Mrs Magpie,
what are you doing here?
I have flown down to spy
if the coast is quite clear.

Tell me, Mrs Magpie,
where's your husband today?
He is nest-building high
where our babies can play.

Goodbye, Mrs Magpie,
I wish you very well.
Good luck, young passerby,
be happy where you dwell.

FELINE WILES

Pussycat faces,
whiskery graces,
           beguile.
Tigerlike paces,
fishy milk traces
          - and smile!

THE CAT DID IT!

Tweety bird met with sudden death,
Sylvester gulped him in one breath.
But that pesky canary bird
Will haunt the cat, you mark my word!
*(I thought I thaw a puddy tat
a-cweepin' up on me...)*

mouse

miniscule creature,

Odd and frisky, whiskery,

Unctious, curious,

Spry and secret in margins,

elephantine in shadow.

Mighty Mouse

Mighty mighty Mighty Mouse!
Wow! He has muscles of steel.
Crunch! He munches blue moon cheese.
Pow! He makes the baddies squeel.

Animal Antics

TOMCAT JERRY

A parody to be read
"jocularly and with the utmost pomposity."

Tomcat Jerry went to Bury.
He clambered up a runner bean,
Then stole a hanky from a pole
And hoped to God he was not seen.
He clawed his way up to Cloud Nine,
Purring: "Jack's beanstalks drip moonshine.
But cream milkshakes, sloshed with sherry,
Will always - hic - keep me merry!"
That was the last time he was seen,
Vanishing up his runner bean.

THE MONKEY

Monkey, monkey, swinging high
In the treetops in the sky,
Are we brothers, are we one,
All together in the sun?

        Who gave you that frame so frail?
        Who made you that curling tail?
        Why have you such puffy cheeks?
        Why such scratches and such shrieks?

Do you wonder why the fuss?
Do you give a thought to us?
Funny, cute and somewhat queer,
Warm and furry, full of cheer.

        When you leap from tree to tree
        Are you glad that you are free?
        You are nimble, you are quick,
        You are up to every trick.

Human hands mark you our kin.
Monkey mischief makes us grin.
If I could I would erase
All the sadness from your gaze.

        Monkey, monkey, swinging high
        In the treetops in the sky,
        We are brothers, everyone,
        All together in the sun.

Pride Shot

Lions were posing for cute pictures.
"Where's your pride?" roared the jungle hectors.
    But the pride shook their manes:
        "Our main concern remains
That our tales be shot, so no lectures!"

PAPER TIGERS

The paper tigers are news deciders,
travelling hither,
travelling thither,
tyrants of the Tigris river.
Married to the tigeresses
owning trigger happy presses,
their hides are bound with
papyrii,
their brains embalmed with
stimuli.
Beware the claws
in tiger paws.
Their evil fangs
like daggers hang.
These gossipy strangers
spell scandal sheet dangers.
These tigers are more than horrific,
they're paperishly tigerific.

Animal Antics

MOTHER AND CHILD

Tableau in Nature:
papoose velcroed to mother,
the koala clings.

PROVERBIAL LOGIC

Where there are pandas
there's bamboo, but the converse
is sadly not true.

COWBOY BILLY JOE

Cowboy Billy Joe
Would ride to and fro
Over the range on
His palomino
Cowboy Billy Joe
Was raring to go
To the arena
Of a rodeo
Cowboy Billy Joe
Would throw his lasso
At cattle and calves
Like a Western Pro.
Cowboy Billy Joe
Became a hero.
"And that's no bull!" said
His best amigo

RIDING HIGH

Napoleon
was painted astride a fierce stallion.
The stuffed horse and artist conspired
to give the image his highness desired.

SQUIRRELING

September's squirrel
husbands its acorns against
bone-bare wintry nights.

My Rabbit is Magic

I have got a rabbit
with a funny ...

        (a) carrot
        (b) grin
        (c) habit
        (d) bone

She twitches her pink nose
and scratches with her ...

        (a) whiskers
        (b) toes
        (c) eyes
        (d) fur

She hops about our home
and fights the garden ...

        (a) gate
        (b) cat
        (c) gnome
        (d) worm

Then bows and, just like that,
she pulls me from her ...

        (a) ears
        (b) hutch
        (c) pocket
        (d) hat!

INSECTS RULE

The birds are all gone
and the insects have
laid claim to the air.

The fish are all gone
and the insects have
laid claim to the seas.

The mammals are gone
and the insects have
laid claim to the land.

The creepy crawlies
have inherited.

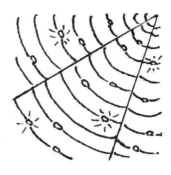

Flat Share

You may think I'm lazy
since I don't dust my flat.
But I love the spiders
that share my habitat.

My windows are grimy
and there's rust on the lock,
providing privacy
to arachne livestock.

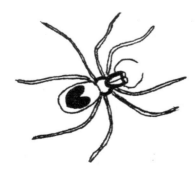

No Chrysalis

Fragile wings testing the air,
we are born beautiful.
But we grow larvaed layers
that harden.

People are not like butterflies.

Study Subject

At the Dinosaur
Museum you can study
Little boys and girls.

THE HIPPO

On the day the hippo stubbed his toe
a kindly magpie chirped: Oh my!
and a hyena laughed: Oo aah!
He got a hug from a water bug,
a pat on his back from the wolf pack,
cocoa and care from a polar bear,
oodles of sympathy from poodles,
but the hippo just gave an almighty BELLOW!

Animal Antics

Astro-turtle

I am the astro-turtle hurtling through space.
Forget the rabbit's habit of losing the race,
No tortoise or porpoise can whizz through my black hole.
Hedgehogs and frogs, tadpoles and moles, don't know my goal.
I am the astro-turtle hurtling through space.

I am the astro-turtle hurtling through space,
Mapping Martian hills and charting Jupiter's face.
Komodo dragons can't hitch their wagons to mine,
Starfish just fade and wish they had my cosmic shine.
I am the astro-turtle hurtling through space.

I am the astro-turtle hurtling through space.
Jelly fish will belly flop, as I soar with grace.
Alligators are just gaping agitators,
Mere imitators of astro-navigators.
I am the astro-turtle hurtling through space.

I am the astro-turtle hurtling through space.
Newts descend in parachutes to find their humble place,
Salamanders salute a commander like me
And lizards in blizzards blink at my majesty.
I am the astro-turtle hurtling through space.

Wisdom Tooth

Ali the Alligator
muttered and his teeth chattered,
a certain indicator
that he had a quite absurd
and most illogical fear
of having a tooth pulled out.
When he made his reason clear,
the friendly dentist gave a shout:
"Wisdom is not found in teeth,
and your wisdom tooth must go.
You will still have brains beneath
your skull and sharp teeth below."
So Ali smiled, he opened wide
and let the dentist look inside.

The Yeti

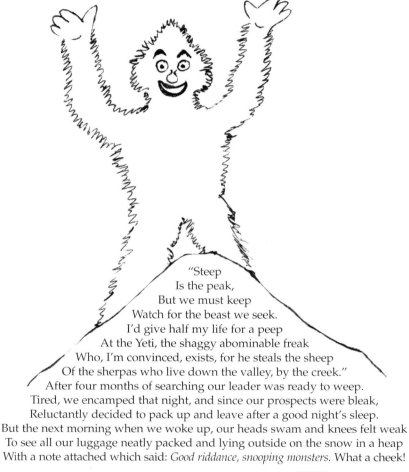

"Steep
Is the peak,
But we must keep
Watch for the beast we seek.
I'd give half my life for a peep
At the Yeti, the shaggy abominable freak
Who, I'm convinced, exists, for he steals the sheep
Of the sherpas who live down the valley, by the creek."
After four months of searching our leader was ready to weep.
Tired, we encamped that night, and since our prospects were bleak,
Reluctantly decided to pack up and leave after a good night's sleep.
But the next morning when we woke up, our heads swam and knees felt weak
To see all our luggage neatly packed and lying outside on the snow in a heap
With a note attached which said: *Good riddance, snooping monsters*. What a cheek!

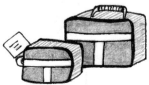

ANTON, THE ANT-EATER

Anton, the ant-eater of Old Canton,
Ate all the ants he could stick his tongue on.
    He'd push through his snout.
    His eyes would pop out
And Anton ate ants until all were gone!

HANGING AROUND

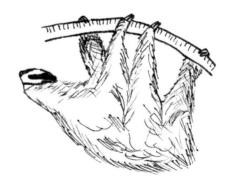

I cling to a tree
and hang high and low.
You have to agree
I'm taking things slow.

Some say I'm slothful
for I'm always found
keeping my hands full
just hanging around.

MELA MENAGERIE

    It was summertime,
the animals were having a mela.
    The elephants cooked
curried pumpkin with *tikka masala*,
    sun-shy frogs and mice
sheltered under the hood of a cobra,
    bears and cockatoos
swapped couplets in a mini *mushaira*,
    horses and camels
pranced and danced a fantastic bhangra,
    tigers took pot shot
at juicy papayas for one paisa,
    lions showed off paws
decorated with delicate henna,
    donkeys for a laugh
crowned Mule their day-long Maharaja,
    pelicans swallowed
swords with mango chutney and *paratha*,
    Sinbad's ship sailed in
on waves of dolphin abracadabra,
    monkeys built bridges
recalling how they once helped Prince Rama,
    while Ali Baba
and forty rooks acted out life's drama.
    It was summertime,
the animals were having a mela.

Animal Antics

HELPFUL HINTS

This collection of themed poetry is a valuable resource for schools and will help promote literacy skills. Children enjoy poetry for its meaning, sound, pattern, unusual expression, beauty and humour. So it is important that the poems in this book are read aloud as well as seen on the page. The extent to which children explore and appreciate content and form also needs checking. They may find some unfamiliar words and, where these are not explained in the book, children should be encouraged to adopt a guided self-help approach to resolving such problems.

Some of the poems in this book are examples of particular forms of poetry. Children can learn to recognise these forms. 'The Yeti' for instance, is a shaped poem, while 'Please Save the Porcupine' is a punning poem, 'Cowboy Billy Joe' is a ballad, 'The Talking Parrot of Timbuktoo' is a limerick, 'Diwali' and 'mouse' are acrostics, 'Riding High' is a clerihew, 'When the Beast Cried' is one of several rondelets, 'Feline Wiles' is a lai or virelai, 'The Monkey' and 'Tomcat Jerry' are parodies of William Blake's 'The Tiger' and Edward Lear's 'Mrs Jaypher' respectively, 'The Cat Did It!' is an epitaph, and 'Squirreling' and 'Mother and Child' are among examples of haiku. Many of these types of poetry are enjoyable and stimulating for children to attempt to write for themselves. Puns and acrostics are always fun. After looking at the mountain peak framing 'The Yeti' and the curvey adder shape of 'Aching Bones', children could attempt poems in interesting shapes such as stars or a crescent moon. They could try thinking up short poem-proverbs along the lines of 'Jumbo Haiku Proverbs', although the strict syllable count of the haiku need not be adhered to. 'The Cat Did It!' features an animal cartoon duo, Sylvester and Tweety, who are always at loggerheads. Children can be asked if they know other pairs of cartoon animals, e.g. Tom and Jerry, and after a discussion about the characteristics of the two, they can try a short poem to illustrate the nature of their relationship.

Poems based on fairy tales, legends and classic stories, e.g. 'The Charming Wolf' based on the story of 'Little Red Riding Hood' and 'Jungle Truth' based on Kipling's story about Mowgli, can sometimes offer a fresh insight to a familiar story. 'Rats in Hamlyn' invites the reader to compare the rats in Hamlyn with the cheating humans who "ratted" on their promise to the Pied Piper; while 'When the Beast Cried' draws attention to issues of beauty, ugliness, vulnerability and tenderness.

In reading the poems, children will inevitably learn something about animals, but also about the multicultural world we live in. 'Mela Menagerie' will make them aware of an increasingly popular summertime festivity in our inner cities. South Asian melas, like Caribbean carnivals, are here to stay. The bhangra, a lively Punjabi dance, has been influencing mainstream dance and music for some time, and multilingual *mushairas* (Arabic for 'gatherings of poets') enrich the literary scene, while Indian foods like *tikka masala* and *paratha* contribute hugely to our gastronomic enjoyment. 'Diwali' is a celebration of the Hindu festival of light, when Lakshmi, the Goddess of Wealth and Good Fortune, flies over the world on her owl and blesses the homes where lamps are lit in her honour. *Rangoli* patterns are drawn at the entrance to a home to welcome visitors, and children will enjoy drawing their own vivid *rangoli* designs on paper. *Diyas* (little oil and cotton wick lamps that are especially lit at Diwali) are also fun to make with coloured plasticene. Diwali is also a festival to celebrate the return to Ayodhya of Rama and Sita, and the triumph of good over evil. *Jai Sita Rama* at the end of 'An Epic Abridged' is a mantra or chant for repetition. It means: 'Victory to Sita and Rama'. Narrative poems like 'An Epic Abridged' can teach about plots and

Animal Antics

interest children in both reading and writing stories. 'Vishnu's Eagle' is about the bird-man, Garuda, who carries Vishnu the Saviour on his back. 'Riding High' will inform the reader that Napoleon was rather small in build but, like many people, when it came to being painted, he was given additional height by being seated on a dummy horse! Some poems may also give rise to useful discussion. For instance, after reading 'Proverbial Logic', 'Please Save the Porcupine', 'Insects Rule' and 'Pride Shot', children can discuss endangered species.

There are several poems about elephants, reflecting the author's bias towards them. Children will be interested to talk about their own pets and favourite animals. They should be asked to observe them carefully and describe them in detail, not just the physical appearance of the stick insect for instance, but also its habitat and food, how it moves and what might be its reaction in a given situation. The different senses can be enlisted to describe the chosen animal - what does it look like? Sound like? Feel like to touch? Perhaps even to smell and taste?

Children will enjoy looking for other examples of animal poems. They can also be asked in groups to collect poems about specific animals, perhaps focusing on their favourite mammals, or rare or extinct animals, e.g. the dodo, or mammals, or reptiles, or insects, or wild animals, or farmyard animals or mythological animals. These poems can be copied out and illustrated. Children will also enjoy sharing these poems with others and should be encouraged to say what they particularly like about the poems. They should also be encouraged to read them aloud, to explore the possibilities of using sound effects (perhaps animal noises and even music) and gestures and movements to dramatise appropriate poems, and to memorise poems that they like.

Animal Antics

ABOUT THE POET

Debjani Chatterjee was born in India and grew up in Japan, Bangladesh, Hong Kong and Egypt. She now lives in Sheffield. She is a writer, editor and storyteller; and frequently runs writing workshops and gives readings in the UK and abroad. She is a member of various writers' organisations, including the Poetry Society, the National Association of Writers in Education and Mini Mushaira. She has had many pets in the past: fish, parrots, budgerigars and dogs; but has always wanted an elephant.

INDEX OF FIRST LINES

The wolf could talk 6
In our school, Miss Meacher 6
The Piper played 7
When the Beast cried 7
Out of thunder 8
Every ocean mermaid had come to masquerade: 9
Diwali lamps are twinkling, twinkling 10
In *Ramayana* 11
Dancing Ganapati, trunk in the air, 12
There's nothing badder 13
In the elephant 14
All trunk, ears and legs, 14
I am the talking parrot of Timbuktoo; 15
Elephants were not her cup of tea - 16
Mowgli grew up in the jungle, 17
One year in the Monsoon season 17
Once a parrot and a goldfish 18
When mates boast about their hamsters, 19
Noah is a boa constrictor, 20
It's like an arm: 20
A sharp-beaked hunter of the chase, 21
Hello, Mrs Magpie, 22
Pussycat faces, 23

Animal Antics

Tweety bird met with sudden death, 23
miniscule creature, 24
Mighty mighty Mighty Mouse! 25
Tomcat Jerry went to Bury, 26
Monkey, monkey, swinging high, 27
Lions were posing for cute pictures, 28
The paper tigers, 29
Tableau in Nature, 30
Where there are pandas, 30
Cowboy Billy Joe, 31
Napoleon 32
September's squirrel 32
I have got a rabbit 33
The birds are all gone 34
You may think I'm lazy 35
Fragile wings testing the air, 36
At the Dinosaur 36
On the day the hippo stubbed his toe 37
I am the astro-turtle hurtling through space 39
Ali the Alligator 40
Steep 41
Anton, the ant-eater of Old Canton, 42
I cling to a tree 42
It was summertime, 43

Other books for children by Debjani Chatterjee

The Elephant-Headed God & Other Hindu Tales
The Monkey God & Other Hindu Tales
Sufi Stories From Around the World
Nyamia and the Bag of Gold
The Most Beautiful Child
The Message of Thunder & Other Plays
The Snake Prince & Other Folk Tales From Bengal

Other books for children from Pennine Pens

Me, Mick and M31 by Andrew Bibby, with teaching pack
Full details of Pennine Pens publications at:
www.penninepens.co.uk